Have you ever been to Kuban?
Try and see yourself
Wonderful people
Famous land

MY NAME IS Kuban

The Caucasus with its rich natural resources and its ideal geographical location has always been an area of great interest to Russia and to some Western European Countries.

In order to strengthen the Russian State in 1711, Peter the First began a long and exhausting war with Turkey for the Black sea and Azov area.

And only under Katherine the Second were the lands occupying the right bank of the Kuban river were finally annexed to Russia.

On January 16, 1778 General Suvorov came to Kopyl, Kuban to provide for the security of the Russian Southern border. He headed the construction of five big fortresses and 20 smaller premises which served the defensive purpose.

On January 16, 1792 General I. Gudovich, an army commander-in-chief in the Caucasus and Kuban, presented Katherine the Second with the plans for the Caucasian military line where he suggested building more fortresses and starting new settlements.

Throughout all the subsequent history, the state interests of Russia have always been completely in tune with the desires of the Black Sea Cossack Army (Voisko).

On February 29, 1792 the Cossack delegation led by Anton Golovaty, an army judge, set off for St. Petersburg with the intention of getting permission to move to the Kuban lands.

Having received the gift certificate (gramota) Zakhary Chepiga, one of the atamans, sent 847 Cossack settlers from Buga to Taman.

On August 25, 1792 a fleet of 50 rowboats and a sailing boat led by Savva Bely, a colonel, landed in Taman. Chepiga himself together with the Cassock Army headquarters, the carts, the Cossack families, with three cavalry and two infantry regiments of more than 2000 people, reached the river of Kuban on May 18, 1793.

The rest of the Cossacks were brought there by A. Golovaty, an army judge, from the end of June through beginning of May, 1793.

Z. Chepiga with the army headquarters pitched a camp in Karasynsky Kut not far from Orekhovo Lake. On June 12, he sent a letter to Judge Golovaty: "My congratulation on the arrival in Taman, a military land. I intend to inform you that I've put the border guards along the river of Kuban and have settled down with my headquarters alongside this river in Karasynsky Kut where I've found a suitable place for a military settlement... "

It was the moment when the Black Sea Cossack decided to start erecting a main town in honour of Katherine the Second, the Great Empress with the construction of a headquarters office and 40 houses.

This is how Ekaterinodar, at that time a military town, was started and began to grow.

Boundless pastures, small and large rivers, lakes with water fowl, steppes covered with vegetation, and rich forests inspired hunting, fishing, cattle breeding and farming which would take a lot of effort and time.

New settlers experienced shortage of bread and some industrial products

during their first years of settlement That was one of the reasons for the rapid fair trade development Ekaterinodar became a centre of busy good exchange. The fairs attracted not only local people but also setters from the other Russian regions and Adyghes from neighbourhood area. The exchange yards were organised in order to develop the trade contacts between Russia and Adygheya. The goods brought from Adygheya became an important part of Cossack trade.

By 1826 on the banks of the Kuban river there were 6 exchange yards established. Shapsughi would always consider the trade with Russia more beneficial than the one with Turkey because from Russia they could get everything they wanted in exchange for timber, cattle and bread. Shapsugh would prefer a peaceful development of their relationship with Russia.

The mutual interest in the further development of this relationship was so great that it would help to tackle all the hindrances put up by the bureaucratic system. The growing trade contacts contributed a lot to the friendship between the Russian and the Adygheya people.

Since then there have been very many historic events taking place in the Kuban land. Some of them were encouraging, but some of them were frustrating. So many different people's fates - distinguished and ordinary, heroic and winning. All of them invested a lot in the area's development.

Time is still creating History nowadays. Kuban Cossacks still remain the foundation for peace and prosperity in the area.

CABINET PO

54. Екатеринодаръ. Памят. Казачьему войску.

Екатеринодаръ

Красная улица

Екатеринодаръ.
2-е реальное училище.

Екатеринодаръ. Тріумфальная Арка

Екатеринодаръ
улица

Екатеринодаръ
Общій видъ города

Екатеринодаръ. Красная улица

It was the end of the 18th century when the southern steppes of Kuban already a part of Russia, became famous for its rich soil.

Any traveller would be delighted to find that vast valley carpeted with a great variety of grass and flowers in full bloom, with wild birds and animals, and with plenty of burial grounds and horse herds.

Now two centuries later endless Kuban steppe has changed a lot. Ploughed fields have turned into developed landscapes, yet it still pleases everybody with its multifacial overflowing fields though it blooms differently.

Many famous scientists and simple ploughmen have devoted their lives to that land. Tendered by the Southern sun, abundantly watered by May rain, the land keenly catching every farmer's word and secret tries not to disappoint while trying to repay fully for the love and care it has been given.

Prominent
plant breeders of
the time

Member of Academy
P. Lukyanenko
Member of Academy
V. Pustovoit

The country has highly praised
their achievements which still
serve people nowadays.

Member of Academy
M. Khadzhinov
Corresponding Member
G. Galeev

There are more than 100 agricultural crops grown in the Kuban land. One of them is rice. Its presence in the area is dated from the middle of the 19th century. But the real rice-growing development started with the introduction of an irrigation system in the area. Not far from a small village, Tikhovsky, Krasnoarmeysky District was that crop first planted under mass production circumstances. This was when the building of the Kuban rice system and the swift development of the Azov paddy fields started. After a few decades Kuban became a major rice producer in Russia. Krasnodar reservoir, the biggest in the North Caucuses, is the heart of a water supplying complex. It is a material foundation not only for rice growing in the area, but also for cultivating fruit and vegetables in the suburbs of Krasnodar. The reservoir contains 3,1 billion m3 of water

When you have some leisure hours on the Black sea coast don't miss your chance to visit a native land of Soviet Champaign - winery "Abrau-Durso", situated on the picturesque bank of Abrau lake.

The rare pleasure of tasting grape wine, flavoured by the Southern sun, by the warm sea breathing and ancient land energy can't be bettered. One will inevitably discover that the skill of producing rare wines is an art, and people who have mastered it are poets... So...

It took some time before the marvellous vineyards of the Russian Tsar's estate "Abrau-Durso" produced a goodly yield. The famous kinds of grapes were delivered from Germany, Austria, France and the Crimea. In 1890-1895 in "Abrau-Durso" there were wine cellars built at a depth of 90 m. under the ground. Alongside the table wine production, Champaign making was started. In 1896 the first 16 thousand Champaign bottles were laid down for ageing by French wine makers who never revealed their secrets to Russian wine makers.

In 1920 A.M.Frolov-Bagreev laid down 35 thousand bottles using a traditional way of storing them. The result surpassed all expectations. problem The riddle was unravelled. Soviet Champaign Brut tastes wonderfully good and solemn. Nowadays Soviet Champaign is matured for years in the cool maze of underground tunnels, it is an object of wine maker's main concern and care. It is exported to many different countries in the world.

Table and vintage wines of "Abrau-Durso" winery are well-known outside this country. Cabernet Abrau with its velvety taste and pomegranate colour is as good as many of the world famous samples. Riesling Abrau strikes with its lightness and refreshing qualities.

The most well-known among "Kubanvino" wines are table wines - Riesling Myskhako, Riesling Anapa, Riesling Su-Pekh, Cabernet Myskhako, Cabernet Abrau; fortified wines - Madeira, dessert wines - Taman, Cherny Glaza, Uzhnaya Noch and so on; cognacs - Krasnodar (KV), Bolshoi priz (KWK), Kuban (KS). The wine produced by such wineries as "Gelendzhik", "Fanagoria", "Malay Zemlya" will also give you a lot of pleasure.

Kuban is an area of two seas: the Black sea and the Azov sea.

If a local wants to impress a dear guest he would take him to see the Azov sea with its beautiful coastline so prized for its hunting and fishing opportunities.

Azov sea modern ichthyofauna contains more than 100 fish species including white sturgeon, stellate sturgeon and sturgeon.

In order to protect and to develop fishing trades in the Azov sea basin a number of fishing farms produce sturgeon, roach and other species for breeding. The Azov sea with its scenic coast and estuaries remains well-known for its fish.

usiness people from all over the world express more and more interest in Kuban, with its resources and prospects. Representatives from more than 60 countries invest their capital into its regional economic development. And it is understandable. Its ideal geographical position, the richness and the variety of its resources, its scientific potential, and its well-developed consumers' market are good guarantees of further economic development.

Kuban has a door to the seas and the World Ocean via such ports as Novorossiisk, Tuapse, Sochi, Eysk, Port Kavkaz, and Temruk.

Three hundred world ports in India, Cuba, Japan, Australia, America and Africa welcome big ocean tankers and bulk carriers from Kuban ports.

Kuban is also a big railway junction in the South of Russia.

There is important freight traffic of oil, oil products, timber, grain, cement and some equipment.

The biggest airports in the region are Krasnodar, Sochi and Anapa airports.

They transport cargo and passengers and can accommodate modern aircraft .

In a word, Kuban has all the potential for prosperity and development in the future.

Our memories are holy...

The horrible events of the Great Patriotic War are all in the past now, but the valorous deeds of its heroes are not forgotten. In August, 1942 the 4th Kuban Cossack Cavalry Corps guardsmen fought to the death defending the Caucuses Gate. The 30th Irkutsk red Banner Division became famous after its battle for the Kuban capital. In September, 1942 Novorossiisk became an inaccessible fortress. The storm group of brave men with Major Ts. Kunikov in command fought fiercely for 225 days to protect "the little land". The battle for Tuapse went on day and night for 150 days, the heroism was overwhelming. In the spring of 1943 the intense battles in the sky of Kuban finally finished with the complete victory of Soviet aviation. The nazis lost 1100 aeroplanes. A.Pokryshkin, brothers D. Glinka and B.Glinka, and F Fadeev were the most distinguished pilots at the time. In September, 1943 after the "Blue line" break through, the Northern Caucasus Fleet steadfastly freed the Black sea coast and Taman. The partisans took an active part in the fight against the occupying forces.

The heroic deeds of our fellow-countrymen have become a significant part of our history. Grand memorials and monuments are a symbol of the eternal gratitude for their unparalleled heroism.

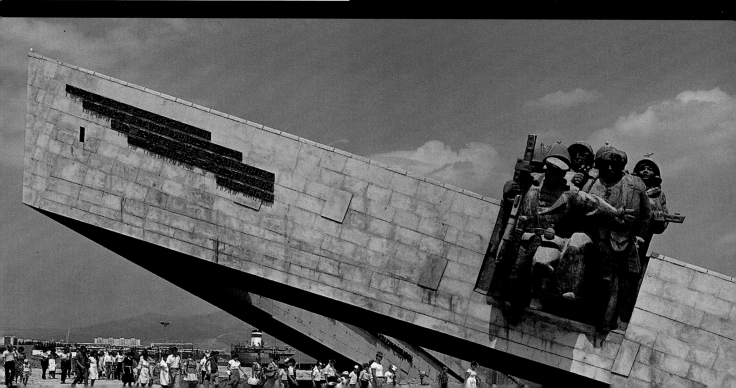

Bust-monument to Marshal G. Zhukov.

Temruk memorial complex

Krasnodar is an Orthodox centre of Kuban.
There is a Krasnodar and Novorossiisk eparchial
board and a few active cathedrals: St. Katherine,
St. Trinity, St. George and some other parishes.
The festive services, ceremonies and spiritual
music concerts are held by the priests and church
members in order to celebrate the important
events of Russian Orthodox Church life.

On June 12, 1993 Ekaterinodar-Krasnodar celebrated its 200th anniversary. The city reached this glorious date with the multi-national population of 764.000 people. Now Krasnodar is an administrative centre with a diverse economy, and is also a big industrial and cultural centre of the Region.

There are dozens of research and design institutes working for the Regional economy. Higher education establishments of Krasnodar are big educational and research centres that provide the foundation for the successful specialists' training in many different fields. They have a wide network of scientific laboratories and libraries. Kuban State Agricultural University, Polytechnic University, Kuban State University, Kuban State Academy of Medicine, Academy of Culture and Arts, and Academy of Physical Training and Sports play an important role in Russian scientific and cultural development.

Krasnodar Regional Scientific Library, named after A. Pushkin, boasts 1,5 million volumes available for its readers.

The oldest Rimsky-Korsakov musical college trains some musicians and vocalists every year. A lot has been done in the regional centre to promote awareness of art and music.

The "Kuban Musical Spring" festival and "Ekaterinodar Musical meetings" are held annually. But the theatre still appeals to Krasnodar audiences most of all. One will see a well-staged performance at the M. Gorky Drama Theatre, the Musical Theatre, or the Puppet's Theatre.

The Centre of Folk songs founded by G.Ponomarenko, a composer, gives regular concerts preserving folk song traditions.

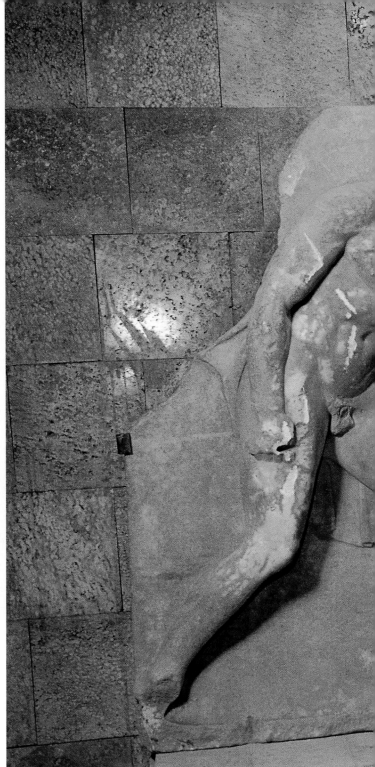

Kuban is a land of ancient civilisations with the ancient culture. It was 2500 years ago when the area of the Kuban river and the Sea of Azov was populated by Meotians, the Taman peninsula was occupied by Sindi, and the first Ancient Greek colonies appeared.

One of the strongest Greek states in the South of Russia was a Bosporian Kingdom with its cities established where there were convenient harbours for ships to dock and rich fertile soil for growing crops.

The art treasures of an Ancient civilisation were discovered in the burial grounds in the South of Russia. They tell us a lot about extinct ancient people, their culture, their customs and their traditions.

During 1Y-Ш centuries BC, the antique cities and states experienced the period of their highest prosperity and most rapid cultural development. The luxurious Tsar Palaces and Cathedrals, were opulently decorated with colonnades, and spacious squares with statues.

Phanogoria, Hermonassa, and Gorgippia are situated in the Asian part. Kostromsky, Ulsky, Kelermes, and Semibratny burial grounds have become famous worldwide because of the unique finds of exceptional scientific and artistic significance. The Krasnodar State historical - archeological Felitsen's museum hosts and exhibits original samples of art pieces made of gold which possess a big artistic and historical value. There are also some cult and everyday items produced by craftsmen.

The Kovalenko Art Museum is famous for its big collection of Russian and Western-European art pieces. The display of Russian art starts with XY-XYII century icon exhibition. In the museum halls there are canvases of XY11- XX century Russian the most distinguished artists. Renaissance Italian paintings, Dutch, French and German paintings of XY11 - X1X century are an object of great interest. The museum keeps rare collections of drawings and porcelain of Russian and Western European artists, and a unique collection of Japanese drawings. The Museum exhibits art pieces from some private collections and from the museums of other countries, and conducts some educational programmes. The Fine Arts Exhibition Hall attracts very many of Krasnodar citizens.

If you have a chance to visit Adygheya you will not be disappointed. Scenic mountains, gorges, gardens and fields, rapid rivers... That's the land of Adygheya. The area is wonderfully beautiful. But the most unforgettable part will always be meeting people. The hospitality, kindness and wisdom of local people with their ancient culture, their love of the land, their customs and traditions, their catchy songs and dances do attract guests and help to develop mutual understanding and long lasting friendships. You are a guest, but you will always feel at home there, comfortable, relaxed and uplifted. That is the secret of Caucasian hospitality.

The Kuban musical art is well recognised and multifaceted. The Kuban state Cossacks' Choir conducted by V.Zakharchenko, a Professor, a State Prize-winner, is well-known all over the world. The Folk Culture Centre of Kuban was opened in conjunction with this professional company. It caused some tangible changes in the cultural life of the Region.

Christmas and Easter Holiday concerts became a tradition together with charity concerts and Musical weeks for children. The Centre's experimental music school for children became a prize-winner and got the 1st prize diploma at the International Competition held by UNESCO. The centre also conducts some all-around activities which include mostly research work in the field of Fine Arts and concert performances.

The Regional Philharmonicy unites such musical groups as the Krasnodar chamber choir, the State Chamber Orchestra of Kuban, the State Song and Dance Company "Cossack Volnitsa" and so on.

In Krasnodar there is a municipal Palace of Art and a Municipal Concert Hall where one can listen to concerts of majestic organ music. The musical show-theatre, the Kuban symphonic orchestra, the Classical Dance Company, Opera Studio, the band, the school of choreography, the puppet theatre, the former actors' theatre were all formed by Fine Arts Company "Premiere". The company is famous for its concerts outside the region.

What a wonderful scenery...
And how appealing the unknown is
How much joy there will be...
And sweet memories...

Water fowl hunting is most popular. A hunter can really experience so many different feelings while duck hunting from a boat or with a hound in August.

How much pleasure one can get sitting in the small hours on the river, watching a beautiful drake in its spring feathers flying lower and lower in circles over the reach being attracted by its crafty female friend.

All this sounds like a wonderful symphony...

The "Turkish fountain" in the suburbs of Taman is an unquestionable example of the depth of human experience. There has been a cold spring there in the sand for 300 years.

Specialists believe that the spring gets its waters not only from the precipitation but also from the condensed moisture. During archaeological excavations of ancient culture layers, structures of crushed stone with embedded clay pipes for providing water during a drought were found. The humidity from the sea air and the moisture from the upper soil layers penetrate the sand where the temperature is much lower than on the ground surface. The amount of moisture collected in the sand and on the pipe walls can be so considerable that it can become an inexhaustible source of water.

About life, about eternal movement high in the sky does the lark sing its song, the sun pours its bright playful rays on the Earth, and the Earth... There is so much charm and marvellous beauty, lively play and highest harmony in it, everything is completely in tune...
Nature is full of poetry...

The Krasnodar Territory is situated in the North West Caucasus. It covers an area 400km from the North to the South, and 360 km from the West to the East. The Northern and Central Parts of the Northwest Caucasus are occupied by the Kuban Valley, and the Southern part consists mainly of Big Caucasus mountains.

The diversity of landscapes hardly matched anywhere else is a unique feature of the area. Wondrous harmony between the boundless steppe and foothill woodlands, the eternal snow capping the Caucasian peaks, the rapid rivers flowing down through the gorges and the deepest caves. What a richness of flora and fauna.

There is a Caucasus State National Park in the area. The scientific and natural complex covers 263,5 thousand hectares of land and is a part of the National Park International Network.

The Northern-West Segment of the Big Caucasus Chain covered with eternal snow capped peaks which go up above the forest zone belongs to the National Park as well.

The High mountain nature is wild and severe in its greatness.

There are many lakes in the Krasnodar Territory. They are a source of water and they also serve as bird habitats. Some salty lakes have healing mud in them. The mountain lakes of the Caucasus draw you with their rare beauty.

Everything is so peaceful and quiet here... The water blinds you with its blue colour and you can breathe so easily. The mountain lakes are the most unforgettable and scenic spots to visit.

Mountain massif Chugush is a place where you can find plenty of bears, deer, chamois and Caucasian goats.

Caucasian goat and chamois herds can only be seen on the mountain tops. They move among cliffs and rocks easily reaching the inaccessible mountain tops with their precipices.

Along the wooded paths and further in the forest wolves, foxes, bears, badgers, hogs and martens lead their own lives.

A Caucasian deer wanders on its own or with a few others. It spends its winters in the deciduous forest, and in the spring-time it goes up into the mountains. In summer it can be found in the Alpine meadows with its spectacular head decoration.

A bison, the tsar of bulls, also moves from the forest zone to the Alpine meadows seasonally. In summer they set off to the mountain ridges which attract them with the coolness of the mountain air and the distinguished grass taste.

The best time to visit Krasnaya Polyana is during the summer and the first days of autumn when you can explore the most untouched mountain slopes covered with the primeval forest and the Alpine meadows.

In winter it is the best place for skiing with its most enjoyable quietness and the freshness of the mountain air.

When the snow starts to melt bears come out of their dens. For a while they prefer to keep to the southern slopes, staying in the sun. Later with the snow disappearing and the first wild flowers starting to bloom bears tend to wander everywhere in their search for food.
Everything is tightly connected in nature: land and water, plants and soils, glaciers, rocks and the diverse animal world. Everything is united, everything is in complete harmony...

Kuban is the main health resort in Russia. Such big resort cities like Sochi, Anapa, Gelendzhik, Tuapse are situated on the Black Sea Coast.

Beaches, good for swimming, favourable Mediterranean and subtropical climate, affluent southern zone vegetation, healing mud and spas, fresh sea air, rich with oxygen, attract many tourists who want to improve their health. Millions of people come to the Black Sea coast to enjoy the sight of the Caucasus Chain peaks capped with snow, waterfalls, noisily rolling down from the cliff tops, the incredible beauty of the mountain lakes, the Alpine meadows with their striking colours...

Sochi is one of the biggest seaside and spa resorts in the world. There is a Mtsesta resort known for its spas which have been found in the Matsesta, Agura and Khosta river valleys since the ancient times.

Romans, Athenians, and Babylonians came to this place from over the seas. Sochi resort is now successfully competing with such world renowned resorts as Nice and San-Remo.

Sochi is a park city.
Its subtropical colouring is created by its palm trees, magnolias, agaves, red maples and numerous decorative flower-beds.
Sochi dendrarium is both a park and a museum. More than 2500 species of various plants brought from many different countries of the world grow there. The subtropical zone flora is widely represented in the " Southern Plants" park. Every tree in the "Riviera" park possesses some healing qualities. The parks' splendour uplifts the visitors' mood creating favourable conditions for health improvement and proper rest.

At the beginning of the century N. Gundobin, a distinguished Russian scientist, wrote: "Anapa is a first class resort for children. Even Western Europe can feel envious of a place like this".

Due to its location between the sea and the steppe and its warm mildly humid climate, Anapa has become one of best children's resorts. The summer is hot there, but the heat is softened by the sea breezes. Anapa also has a wonderful sand beach. The sea is quite shallow, and its bottom is very gently sloping, so even very small children can swim there.

Healing qualities of the sulphide, silty and volcanic mud of Chembursky and Salty lakes and Vityasevsky liman are important factors that attract tourists as well. The mineral water from the Semigorya and Raevsky area spas can not be found anywhere else in the country. Dzhemete Sulphide water has the same characteristics as famous Matsesta mineral water. Anapa resort is designed to welcome mostly families with children.

Surrounded by mountain ridges on three sides Goryachy Kluch, one of the oldest resort locations, 65 km from Krasnodar occupies a picturesque place in the Northern Caucasus. Its climate is moderately continental with mild winters and warm summers. The resort is rich with spas. The most popular product is the mineral water called "Goryachekluchevskaya". According to the results of gastric-intestinal disease treatment, Goryachy Kluch can easily catch up with such famous resorts as Essentuky, Morshin, Zheleznovodsk and so on.

Our meeting is coming to an end. Our short story about Kuban history and daily life is almost over. The story where we intertwined the problems of everyday needs and eternal beauty, where we mentioned the main aspects of city life and the ever-lasting human desire for progress and growth.

And great nature which will always remain the origin of life and the spiritual source of man's growth. We are one united body with it. Marvellous landscapes, sea swimming, fresh mountain air, spas, birds' singing give us so much pleasure ...

And man has to take care of nature in return for the joy it gives him in order to preserve it in a healthy and robust state for future generations hoping that in the centuries to come Kuban will still surprise visitors with the diverse colourful world of nature, will attract them irresistibly while giving them a wonderful feeling of anticipation and inspiration for the future.